# ENOUGH *is* ENOUGH

Anthony "Marsman" Brown

**BALBOA.**
PRESS
A DIVISION OF HAY HOUSE

Scripture taken from the King James Version of the Bible.

Balboa Press books may be ordered through booksellers or by contacting:

Balboa Press
A Division of Hay House
1663 Liberty Drive
Bloomington, IN 47403
www.balboapress.com
1 (877) 407-4847

Print information available on the last page.

ISBN: 978-1-5043-3872-1 (sc)
ISBN: 978-1-5043-3873-8 (e)

Balboa Press rev. date: 9/30/2015

# Contents

# THE WESTERN BLACKMAN

I am a western black man who is saying <u>Enough is Enough</u>! For centuries, my race have endured brutal pain and suffering all because God created me from black dirt in the image of the Black Christ in the Holy Bible.

Ever since slavery in the western hemisphere, I've read, seen and heard about some wicked things done to the black man by the white man. Years gone by, the white men were said to be the devil because every nonwhite race on earth was oppressed by them. The Chinese and the Indians also felt the brutal hands of the white man and they too have their story.

In this, the 21$^{st}$ century the black man has come a long way. We have travelled a long hard rocky road tainted with the blood of our ancestors to get where we are and the time has now come where we must say enough is enough because there are those who are determined to continue on a path of hatred. Our cups are filled and running over with tears so to put an end to centuries of hostility against us, we have to start working for a better tomorrow because with the kind of racist systems in place there's no better today. We salute our heroes who because of the inspiration of God stood up and led the way to our freedom. People like MARCUS GARVEY, MARTIN LUTHER KING junior, NELSON MANDELA, MALCOLM X and KING HAILE SELASSIE just to name a few, with the latter saving Ethiopia and its people from a vicious attack by the Italian fascist Mussolini who they thought had a superior army. The Chinese will always speak about Chairman Mao Tse Tung and the Indians will speak of Mahatma Gandhi who because of their bold inspired approach to freedom did what most people thought was impossible at that time. Also, we will never forget the reggae music legends led by the great Bob Marley that rocked the entire world beating down the unjust system.

In today's world not all white men is the enemy because there are good ones but sadly, the good ones are so few it's as if none at all exist. All is not lost though because you can see where some of the good white men are actually trying to reach out to us but there is a trust issue involved. Some think that what their fore parents did to our fore parents, we might literally turn on them with the slightest chance we get. Then, those who are hardened with hate have become the perfect hypocrites. In addition, only those prejudice white men still refer to the black men as a "NIGGER" but strangely, how many of the white women refer to us that way? The white racist man has to remember that the black man has all right to be here just like him because our fore parents worked for centuries building the Western Hemisphere and was never paid a red cent! The prejudice white man also has to remember that the black man went to the battlefront and defended this country with his life so the black man owes him NOTHING! One also has to remember that during wars, the black soldier had to fight his battle outside of a ditch because the white man wouldn't allow him into the same ditch to take cover from enemy attack.

With all that was said and done sometimes I wonder why we have to be the ones who are always compromising but then again we have to go strictly by what the black Christ teaches in the Holy Bible, to love God, your neighbor and even your enemies. Read (Matthew Chapter 5 vs 43-48 and Matthew Chapter 22 vs 34-40). We have to show that we are bigger and better than all this wickedness and let bygones be bygones because we cannot change the past. We cannot allow generations after generations to come into this world filled with nothing but hate all because of a person skin color. We did not create ourselves so we have to show respect to our creator who created man in His own image, by building foundations with nothing but love and forgiveness so future generations black and white can live in unity. In spite of everything we have been through, going from being **Israelites** in the Holy Bible to this sorrowful Godforsaken life and being the victim of the worst identity theft known to mankind, we are sometimes our own worst enemy and have been that way for centuries. Some of us blame the white folks for everything but we have to remember the roles we played in selling blacks into slavery and assisting the wretched slave master on the slave plantation in keeping blacks into slavery. During those miserable days, we were denied the rights to basic education where we were kept ignorant and deliberately kept out of schools. This ignorance poured over in our lives even today because most of the problems we face in the community it's because of it. Today, education is accessible to all races with few interruptions and thank God there are now laws to protect your rights. We keep forgetting that all our freedom fighters shared one thing in common, that education is the only tool that will take the black race forward. The more educated you are, is the more confident you'll feel. You will be well set to earn top salaries at the work place and you will be more respected. But there's a serious problem because every time some of us find ourselves being educated at a certain level or start making money in abundance we start to feel that we have arrived so we stop looking into the mirror and start to look down on our fellow black man hence, forgetting our culture. The great Marcus Garvey said that if you don't know where you came from you won't know where you are going and that statement should be taught to all our children so that they will unite and respect each other. Some of us also have the tendency to make our black women feel inferior by chasing after white women every time we get successful. This is a clear case of not remembering where we are coming from and it's a shame because if you were still poor, she wouldn't have anything to do with you. For those who believe in God and the Holy Bible, there is no place in society today for a bigot and there's no advantage for one race over the other. Read (Romans ch.10, vs 11-13) and there is evidence of that when there is a natural disaster, no one is spared, black, white, rich or poor.

# THE TRUTH MATTERS

We are now in a situation where the chains have been removed from our hands and feet but it is now wrapped firmly around our minds with no chance of liberation soon. We are a race that is mentally weak and for us to be mentally strong we cannot do it without making a distinction between the true black Christ of the Holy Bible and the false blue eye white Jesus that the white man brought about during slavery to keep us enslaved. Remember our inspiration must come from the Holy Bible that teaches us in the Commandments that we should put no other god before the Black Christ who took the Israelites out of bondage in Egypt. Read (Exodus Ch. 20 vs 3-6). Also, the black Christ our Messiah is the same one who took us from the gruesome reality of slavery here in the western hemisphere and we should be ever thankful. We have been asleep for far too long and too trusting of people who are wise and wicked and mean us no good. This is the time for us to wake up because physically, we are the strongest race and slavery is testimony to that. No other race on earth could survive the brutal onslaught that the black race endured for so many centuries. The Olympics is also proof of our physical strength and endurance. Apart from physical strength, we are equally talented in everything you can think of in society once we get exposure and you don't have some bigot trying to keep you down. Some of us are too laid back, sadly thinking that cool breeze is always at our trails and not understanding the type of evil that we are up against, hence, we always take the whole situation for granted when we are dealing with **people who don't like us, never did and never will like us.**

We have to remember that the Chinese and the Indians were also oppressed by the white men but they have totally liberated themselves both physically and mentally. The Chinese economy is the strongest in the world and the Indians have the world fastest growing economy as we speak. When you have a nation that is economically strong the lives of their people will drift further and further away from poverty so without a doubt they are on their way to prosperity.

The Chinese and Indians did not reach where they are only by hard work because no race on earth worked harder than the black race who without a doubt is going nowhere in life with their present state of mind and attitude. The Chinese and Indians are where they are because of their strong spirituality. They believe that they have a strong connection to God in their own way and who are we to disbelieve them when we can see the results of their efforts. There is a very important part of their spirituality, their God looks exactly like them and not like someone else so at all times they feel appreciated and in oneness with the Creator so you know the love and respect for their own race will be strong.

With the western black man, a total mental transformation is needed because his God in his mind is white, God chosen people in his mind is white and what the slave master taught his fore parents years ago during slavery and passed down to him through his descendants, he believes that it is superior to what is written in the Holy Bible. As long as they keep seeing a picture of what they believe is God as white they are going to see the white man as superior and that is the psychological disadvantage they put themselves in.

The black man only hope is the truth of the Holy Bible, the Church and The Black Christ who established the Church but it's going to be a very tall order because some little misguided black pastors who claims that they run Churches and feels that their skin color is not good enough to be associated with God is one of the black man biggest problem and they are the ones that get full approval and appreciation from the prejudice white man. It is said that a picture says a thousand words and when the Holy Bible teaches you about the Black Christ and you have this brain wash distraction pushing into the black family faces every time they enter a Church then that's a serious crime against people who have been beaten and battered down into submission. I don't care what color the prejudice white men want to paint their Christ in because one thing I know for sure the Holy Bible does not lie so definitely their information must be coming from something else that is trying to oppose the Great God Almighty. The Church supposed to be the voice of God in any society and those who are head of the Churches in this life is Christ representative, therefore, how they present the Gospel of the Black Christ is uttermost important. These pastors have the responsibility to let the authoritative voice of God be heard through man. No lie or half truth must be entertained. I must remind these little misguided pastors that adding and subtracting from the word of God is one of the Holy Bible greatest sins and those who are in charge will be held to a higher standard from God so they should be very careful that their practice is not keeping a lot of decent black folks away from Christ. Read (James Ch.3 vs1). Why should the black man even enter an institution which is greeting them with a lie? These pastors have to remember that when they learn theology from some colleges and get a degree in theology they are going to pack their brains with twisted truths so when they present the prejudice white man Gospel to Black folks they will actually be conspiring with any white men that want to keep us in line. The argument from these little misguided pastors is that color don't matter. **I totally agree with that**. But the truth matters and God stated specifically in the Holy Bible that He hate LIARS. Read (Numbers ch23 vs19) and (Proverbs ch12 vs 19- 22). How can you say that you represent Christ the Mighty God who can destroy both body and soul and you are so silent about important issues that affects humanity and turn your backs and be afraid of man? The black Christ taught us that when we represent Him and find yourself up against evil forces you must speak your mind openly just like He did. Read (Matthew Ch.23). Also, I am wondering if these misguided pastors realize what the Black Christ meant when He said to deny yourself and take up the cross and follow Him. Read (Matthew ch.16 vs 24-26) and (Luke ch.9 vs 23-27). If they are not prepared to do so they are nothing but little **wimps** who is not worthy of the title that they hold and should step aside! They are people of no faith because what they are actually doing is promoting the prejudice white man claimed superiority which is a lie because the Holy Bible teaches that it's a level playing field at the foot of the cross and it always will.

Has anyone of these black pastors ever wondered why it is so important to the prejudice white man to have the painting of Jesus white when they know the truth of the Holy Bible? Most white men are atheist so why are they spending so much time tampering with the Bible and promoting someone when they don't think the person exist. I wonder sometimes if any of these black pastors ever done a research on the painting of this false blue eye white Jesus, who it really was and the shameful character of the person who painted it. I think they all should and when they finally know the truth they will understand that this picture of this false blue eye white Jesus was nothing but a total distraction hence, they can remove it and let us worship in spirit and in truth just like what the Holy Bible teaches. Read (John Ch.4 vs 24). **WHEN THE RESEARCH IS DONE, WHO ARE WE GOING TO BELIEVE, THE HOLY BIBLE OR MAN?**

# POOR FAMILY STRUCTURE

Most white folks can trace their family ancestry back to Europe and are still communicating with relatives abroad. Our ancestry links with the mother land Africa were broken during slavery and even though we are here in the Western Hemisphere for so many centuries we can barely trace back more than five generations from this day and this is disgusting!

The Holy Bible speaks very strongly about the importance of the family and that is the area in which the black man is failing miserably. Again we see the importance of the teachings of the Black Christ in the Holy Bible. For too long we see the black man not stepping up as the head of the family not offering economic support, not praying with the family so they can stay together and stop going around having children with several different women or running away like frightened rabbits every time a woman says she is pregnant. If you are financially strong then there is no problem having a lot of children if it is only with your wife but when the problem starts is when you have several children with different women and you are not financially strong. Have you ever wondered why the black Christ wants you to stay together as a family? Some of the reasons are: It would be more economical if all your children have the same sir name, live under the same roof, share everything and eat out of the same pot. This could definitely save you the head of the family a lot of money and bring a lot of love and unity in your family. All this poverty that some of us find ourselves in and still trying to bring down more on ourselves could be alleviated if we just do what the Black Christ teaches and control below our waist by not having sex until we are married. This is a grave problem that the black man must learn to conquer because the devil is skillfully using the flesh to destroy our lives.

The whole break down of the black man life started as a young boy growing up in a single family home not having any important father figure around to give moral and economic support. His mother has to go out and do a full time job or jobs to alleviate the financial constraints and in most cases he is left with grandparents, who, sometimes is too old to monitor him so he is left basically on his own. His education while growing up is not up to standard because there is nobody at home to see to it that he does his homework and study. Also, there is nobody to attend PTA meetings and have regular dialogues with his teachers as a means of checking up on him while he is in school. Regular checks must also be made on the type of friends that he associate with because whether you like it or not they could be the biggest distraction. Children that are well monitored by both parents are more likely to do extremely well in school. We just cannot leave his total education up to his teachers alone or the chance will be there for him to become a statistic. **No offence to anyone but teachers just cannot do it alone**.

History has shown that when children are not properly monitored it can be a disaster. The older they get is the more distracted they'll get and their peers will always influence them in a different direction from what they learn at home, not liking school, trying alcohol and pot and in most cases being lead to a life of crime. If they are lucky enough not to be hooked on drugs or expelled from school, they will end up leaving school without a skill or a high school diploma. The way they dress (sag style) which the Chinese and Indians do not entertain and the various things they do to their natural bodies it will be difficult for them to get a job when the time comes so they make life even more difficult for themselves.

When he reaches 18 years of age, he is now a grown black man and you have to pray that the positives that he was taught at home he will remember and live by them. Depending on the condition that he was brought up in, he will or he won't and if he doesn't remember he will not have much love and respect in his heart for anyone. He must be very aware that the United States that he lives in has broken every commandment set down by the black Christ of the Holy Bible and has made this their way of life which they are always trying to impose on other people. Yes, some of them even jump for joy because they have gotten their way around man, and behave as if they have won the battle of opposing the black Christ commandments. What they don't understand is that the commandments of the Holy Bible were set down by God for us to obey and not debate and

God word is final. I hope that these people, some claiming to be Bible scholars will bear in mind that **the great God Almighty has never lost a battle**! Also, the US is filled with racism and because of the type of system in place it will never change so he has to try much harder than the white man if he is going to be successful in life. If he has no job, sometimes when he finds himself being broke, he is going to get aggressive, desperate and frustrated when the system gets to him. He has no one to turn to for help except his peers who are also filled with a lot of anger and in most cases have nothing but negative vibes so the whole situation gets heart breaking.

These are the sort of situations that the black man finds himself in on a day to day basis, (**Poverty, Hardship and Frustration**) and no hope in most cases of being elevated without education. When the harsh reality of life begins to bite, he begins to cast blame on others for his downfall which was partially created by his parents. Parents must shoulder and partially bare some of this responsibility because most of them have turned their backs on the teachings of the black Christ in the Holy Bible. Also, parents are supposed to constantly teach and remind their children of their rich history and not allowing them only to learn the garbage that the white man has to offer in this false blue eye white Jesus that they promote. We have to look into ourselves first before we start to cast blame because for example, if you were in a class with 20 students and 5 students in the same class excelled and went on to get their degrees in various discipline, it clearly means that you did not apply yourself because you all got the same lessons. With all that is said and done, the United States of America has the best system of Governance on paper but because of the racist practice of some of the individuals that manage the system, for any black man to get any form of justice it's like pulling **teeth**. Take a look at what the system does to them when they do not do well in schools. On a population basis in the United States where the black man is the minority, he is disgracefully the majority in the **prisons** and always being targeted by police. We have to remember that education and Godliness goes hand in hand and the more we turn our back on education is the more we turn to crime and prison. The man who supposed to be head of the family and the bread winner according to the Holy Bible finds himself being outnumbered by his black sisters in areas of higher learning, for example the universities. That is quite a commendable achievement by our sisters but we are finding ourselves drifting further away from what the Holy Bible teaches. If the man is going to be the head of the family he has the God given responsibility to educate himself at a certain level where his authority as head of the family will never be questioned. **HE HAS TO STEP UP!**

# HAVE NO PLAN

The difference between the black man and the white man is, most black men has no plan while the prejudice white men are always planning both long term or short term and the only time their plan involves us is when they are trying to shut us out or keep us in line. Some white men are very subtle and claims that they have mastered the art of the mind game so they thinks that in this fast pace world where technology is the order of the day, they are king. Some black men educational standard is below par so the white man is always skillfully using that advantage without most of us knowing to push us back. So again we see how important education is.

Again I must emphasize if we don't have a total mental transformation with the right attitude the black man is going nowhere don't matter how hard some of us try! We were taught by our parents and grandparents to study, pass our exams in school and go and look a job. Unlike the Chinese and Indians who teach their children to study, pass their exams and do business. So we see why they are so successful and thriving economically because their thinking is always above the bar while we are always aiming below the bar. Let's lift the bar so we can compete head to head and create equal opportunity to build our race by stop settling for second best and not afraid to reach for the sky. Nothing is wrong with working for somebody but in working for somebody there is a limit to your earnings that's why the white man can manage to keep us in line. In business especially when you are just starting discipline and patience have to be number one and sky will be the limit for your earnings if you put in the hard work. The Chinese and Indians have learned through education that in order for them to strive they have to remove all the white man garbage out of their minds and move past the white man and look only to themselves for maximum support. We practice the opposite of that where we turn our backs on education and maintain the white man garbage in our minds and continue to support the white man instead of our own people and this is very important especially where business is concerned. Apart from business, there are other important things on the horizon where we are more gifted than all the other races. In entertainment and sports we are number one because of our physical strength whether American football, baseball, basketball or track and field. Approximately ninety percent of sport stars in the US are black and little by little we see more blacks becoming coaches. That's good but the real question, how many blacks own a team? So you see where the real economic strength is. Spectators don't pay their money to see owners perform, yet owners make all the money and have all the big feisty talk especially about our skin color, while we are the ones out there on the field getting fractures. A sports career can be very fragile because if we are not careful, our careers can be cut short because of a serious injury and there is always somebody to replace us.

The white men will take their money and skillfully invests it all over the world and build wealthy empires. Now, there's nothing wrong with that because they are providing vital jobs but we need to take a leaf out of their books and stop putting all the eggs in one basket, their basket. What the white man has did not come overnight so we need to stop waiting on the impossible to happen and start to deal with our problems head on in a realistic way. We have to always remember that they don't like us and they will never accept us as their equal, so we have to stop fooling ourselves and stop running down what the white man is doing and create our own systems. For a better tomorrow, we have to remember that the white man is not going to surrender a piece of the pie just like that so to get our fair share we must start with education. We have to start building our empire elsewhere so all black entertainers and sports men worldwide who make some crazy millions every year must start thinking about investing some of the money they make in the mother land Africa because that is where the true strength of the black man is whether you like it or not. In so doing we are not going to give up our rights of existence here in the western hemisphere to the white man because our fore parents paid the crucial price for us to be here. Remember the great Marcus Garvey called for a United Africa years ago and went to prison for his efforts so your effort now could be the step in the direction of unity. We have to remember that some white men are always planning and somewhere in that plan they are always trying to bring you down so you have to be very careful and very determine to succeed in whatever we do to keep away the evil forces. Also for those who were wise enough to elude the white man traps and retire with their millions from entertainment or sports they are going to try and take away all your money in whatever way they can and we have seen evidence of that.

The white man economic dominance will continue for a long while if we don't start making positive plans now. You have to remember that for them to become rich from sports they need us. We have to stop distancing ourselves from the mother land Africa because evil forces are always at work and they are real and very powerful. We can't tell you how to spend your money but buying large mansions and several expensive motor vehicles with loud music made by the white man can be a distraction because as we said before, one injury can wipe out everything and put you back to square one. Investing in the mother land Africa is a long term plan which will surely bear fruits in the not too distance future for our generations. It's only the blacks who are making crazy millions in whatever discipline they are in that can make this possible. The road we have to travel to achieve our goals will be rocky because the rich, prejudice white man is going to apply a lot of financial pressure and make a lot of demands. But just like our ancestors Shadrach, Meshach and Abednego in the Holy Bible book of Daniels, faced enormous pressure from the devil and didn't surrender to his demands. Their faith in the Black Christ was very strong and when you serve Him and don't put any other god before Him your protection from Him is guaranteed. Once the mother land Africa gets economically strong the life of all the people worldwide will improve tremendously and there can be nothing but love and unity between all races.

Imagine to see that day when people from all over the world will be applying for top of the line jobs in Africa.

Some sure investment opportunities are, (1) the African Continent produces the most talented soccer players in the world today so why don't we invest in building stadiums and start a professional soccer league in the mother land Africa. Soccer is super business and it is the most popular game in the world. People will travel miles and pay any amount of money to see great players perform. We are allowing Europe to be controlling the sport of soccer and they are not producing any quality soccer talent compared to what Africa produces. Look at how baseball, American football and basketball are marketed in the US. China is also promoting a super soccer league in their country and it is a huge success so far. (2) Africa has the best agriculture climate in the world and has the ability to produce top class foods once we start catching and piping water all across the motherland. From as far back as we can remember the great rivers of Africa were never dry so install the pumps and send the water through those pipes to the farms. Africa has the best climate to produce solar power so all your business can be solar driven. It is important to note that if Europe or the US had the type of consistent sunlight that Africa has, they would have fully utilized the sunlight. This will not be an overnight affair so we have lots of grounds to make up but we have to start somewhere and grow with confidence as time passes. The prejudice white man and his false blue eye white Jesus has been embedding in the black man mind for centuries that you can't do this, you can't do that and you will never be good enough. Sadly that garbage have poured over to today where some of us are still believing that we do not look like God and are not worthy enough to enter God's kingdom. The Black Christ of the Holy Bible teaches that all things are possible if we have faith in Him and color is not a factor. Read (Mark Ch. 9 vs 23) (Mark Ch. 11 vs 24) (Matthew Ch. 17 vs 20) (Philippians Ch.4 vs 10-13).

Do not be distracted by the negatives that take place in Africa from time to time because of the prejudice white man evil plan which he is determined to keep just to maintain his economic superiority. Some white men are notorious capturers and the reason why they have been so successful over the centuries is because some of us are **sellouts**. Whatever they get their hands on, they holds on to it for generations so **there's no piece of the pie for the black man in the their world**. In spite of all the distraction over the decades, the African continent is among the top five fastest growing economy in the world today as we speak and the safest place to live when it comes to natural disasters. Also according to history, the Garden of Eden and the Ark of the Covenant that is mentioned in the Holy Bible is buried somewhere in Africa so we all know what this could mean for tourism. The black man outside of Africa has a very important part to play and we cannot afford to fail. Too many of our African brothers and sisters are turning away from the Christian faith and turning to some other religion. This is happening because of the oppressive way Christianity was presented to their ancestors by wolves in sheep clothing. This is where education is important because we have to let them understand that the Holy Bible teaches that **only in Jesus the black Christ there is SALVATION** and the Holy bible does not lie. Read (John Ch. 14 vs 1-7) and (John Ch. 10 vs 1-9). When the white racist man executes his evil plans in Africa he usually works with stupid power hungry oppositions in all the African countries to try to destabilize the economy at all times. This destabilization of the African economy usually brings distrust and disunity among the African people against their governments, which usually causes a military coup and bloodshed. When this happens, they drink champagne and celebrate because they want to convince the African people that they cannot govern themselves. They then prepare themselves to take advantage of the evil situation which they created in whatever way possible to add more riches to their wealth. You want proof, where did these poor African people get these weapons of mass destruction from which cost so much money and they can't even afford to find food. These weapons were not manufactured in Africa so where did they come from?

Another difference between the white man and the black man, the white man always has the most educated in charge of his evil plan and not the muscles or the educated dunce. For too long we see military coups springing up in Africa because of some stupid reasons. The military in Africa must understand that the days of the dictator is finished and they are there to support and take full orders from the political party that is elected by the people. Also, their responsibility is to see to it that elections are peaceful and fair and defend the country with their lives. Elected governments must understand that they are there to serve and not rip off the people who elected them. They must put on the top of their priority list, **PROPERLY EDUCATING THE PEOPLE**. We must never go back to the days where the strongest, meanest man was in charge of a village and the only time you can remove him from power was to fight and kill him. Leadership like that was ungodly and can never be progressive because when you are at the head you have to plan, govern and out think other well educated people from other countries.

Let's take a look at a country called Germany as example. They were torn apart by two world wars, divided by the Berlin wall and occupied by the United States in the west and Soviet Union in the east after the second world war. Approximately fifty years after, the Berlin wall came down and the country was united again. Today as we speak they have the strongest economy in Europe. If nations without the Black Christ of the Holy Bible can be so progressive, then all we have to do is find ourselves on the road to the Black Christ and do GREATER. (Read John CH. 14 vs 12-17) in Holy Bible for the real facts.

# COMMUNITIES

In the United States of America there are thousands of different communities where people call homes. Some communities are mostly populated by whites while others are mostly populated by blacks. Ironically, the ones that are mostly populated by whites are called the white man's heaven and that heaven has always been the black man's hell. The white man can drive or walk around in the black man's community anytime he wishes but when the black man drive or walk through any white man's community either dogs are released on him or police harasses him with him ending up in jail and history have taught you that blacks have been brutalized in some cases.

The great Marcus Garvey one of our greatest black heroes taught us that if we don't know where we're coming from we will never know where we're going. Unlike the Chinese and the Indians who are constantly reminded of their history by their elders, blacks literally know little or nothing about black history. You want proof of that, go into any black community and ask several black teenagers question about the Honorable Marcus Garvey and you will hear the embarrassing answers. Just to give you a little insight, Martin Luther King junior, Minister Farrakhan and Malcolm X learnt from the Honorable Marcus Garvey and other great world leaders including Mahatma Gandhi and Nelson Mandela also benefitted from his teachings.

The great Marcus Garvey said what he admires about the white man is the unity amongst them and from what we have learnt in history they have always appreciated themselves more and remained united to stay on top of the black man. When the Berlin wall came down East and West Germany immediately united. Scotland voted in their referendum to remain a part of the United Kingdom. There's already the United States of America and last but not least we have to remember that there is a president of Europe.

Everywhere you turn you see a united white man, with some taking full advantage of our indiscipline approach to life so how is the black man going to get out of this trapped situation when the trust level amongst blacks is already at an all time low? We fight against each other and try to tear down everything that our black brothers and sisters try to build up. Our only way to redemption is in the black Christ because only through Him we can feel appreciated. In reading the Holy Bible we will learn the way of the Black Christ and defeat greed, selfishness, envy, **bad mind** and weakness of the flesh.

In the white man's community the only time there is division is when it comes to politics or religion but when it comes to color they remain united to stay on top of all nonwhite race. In their community there is always a sense of high security and unity among whites which usually creates peace and tranquility. Most things are smooth sailing where you will see a lot of private roads and warning signs which is definitely for the black man. The only time you see a black man in their community is when they are the maintenance man, the helper or a very rich individual living with a white spouse trying to get acceptance. In some black communities, there's a lot of black on black crimes, drugs, unwanted children, serious poverty and prostitution. The black man did not put himself willingly in this situation, he was born into it and because of that he has to take the bull by the horn and deal with it! When he gets tired and frustrated with the system he turns on himself and this again is where education is important. It's almost impossible to be humble without the Black Christ in this type of situation so the black on black crime is inevitable. If you are not lucky enough to be born with a special talent the word on the street is that he is willing to die trying to get rich and solve his financial problems to get out of poverty. What are we going to do about this type of thinking? We can't tell ourselves that there's no hope and waiting for somebody to be sorry for us while surrendering to an evil system that plagued us for generations. We will never be respected and will always be referred to as a "**NIGGER**" by some white men if we continue to force ourselves into their way of life! **How much more should we bare before we get it?** There is a way out, the Gospel of the Black Christ is the only way out and when you start reading the Holy Bible and trusting in Him everything flows from there including going to school and educating yourselves. Holy Bible reading (Philippians ch.4, vs. 10-14). As long as you listen to some people garbage more than how you read the Holy Bible your life will never improve positively. You will always put yourself at risk of being brainwashed, embarrassed and taken advantage of. The Holy Bible also teaches you that you don't have to be rich to be contended because we have seen where people who are rich have been very unhappy and sometimes committing suicide while we see people who are poor are far more contented and happier. To be happy and contented is to be stress free and we know what stress can do to the entire body. The way of the black Christ will create a stress free life and will make you show love and respect to your neighbor and practice the golden rule of the Holy Bible. What you don't like for yourselves, don't do to others. (Mathew ch.7 vs. 12).

There is a certain practice among blacks in the community that when they get a painful broken heart from especially a bad relationship or a childhood dream about to materialize and is shattered by a wicked decision made from a bigot that goes against them, they get depressed and sometimes run to an antichrist psychiatrist for treatment. This treatment usually cost a lot of money that erodes their hard earned savings. No problem in going to a doctor but what the doctor is going to do is give you a lot of sleeping tablets so you can sleep off the stress which sometimes reaches severe depression without the right treatment. He who feels it knows it and when you experience living in a society that makes your skin color a sin, it will drive up your stress level to a dangerous level. After taking the prescribed medicine, you sleep and wake up hoping that you will forget all the problems but you start remembering things all over again because you can't change your skin color. The bottom line truth is, no doctor without the black Christ has any cure for this kind of sickness but they are not going to tell you that because they love your money. This kind of sickness which can send you straight to the asylum affects you deep down inside where only God can reach so it's best to go straight to the black Christ on your knees with fasting and prayer. The good thing about going to the Black Christ of the Holy Bible, it doesn't cost you a cent. The next mistake the black man can make is when he gets frustrated with the system that always goes against him and he finds himself being hopelessly hooked on hard drugs. When his friends and relatives comes to his rescue and take him to an institution that they claim can wash the drugs out of him and make him brand new in a few weeks without introducing the Black Christ can get nowhere. When he leaves the institution he is going to be pulled back into a situation and start taking hard drugs all over again because he will be vulnerable without the black Christ intervention. You have to remember that what the hard drugs did to him will affect deep inside his mind where doctors cannot reach but only God can. Constant fasting and prayer is the only sure cure and the way of the black Christ will not fail. Don't wait until you get a prison sentence before you decide to come to the black Christ. Trust in Him first and keep all these drastic problems away and remember to read the Holy Bible. Also, you have to remember that the black Christ living condition when He walked with man in the flesh was similar to what we call ghetto today but because of the love that He had, His way of life showed us that ghetto was created in the mind and not in a place. There is no shame in being poor and not having an abundance of things. The Holy Bible teaches that it's better to be poor than be a liar. Read (Proverbs Ch. 19 vs 22). Where the condemnation comes in is when you try to stifle the truth and not live by the words of the black Christ.

# NO PRIDE

The black race has become the most insulted race on earth without even knowing it. We have lost our sense of pride by playing into the hands of the white man far too often. Even some of our light skin brothers and sisters are taking advantage of the situation by rubbing salt into our wounds. We have allowed some of them who refuse to accept that they are black and some white people not accepting them as white to insult us every chance they get. They literally form a middle clique and join with the prejudice white folks to cast some serious insults and abuse at us when we didn't do them anything. What is so shameful about this is we literally take these insults and abuse as invitation.

A well known white designer came on national television and said he designed his clothes for whites only and not for blacks to wear. In spite of this dreadful insult we just don't get it in our heads and still continue as we speak to buy and wear his clothes from the white man store and making them very rich. A KKK member designed something looking like a crown where people stuck to their car dash board filled it with air freshener and mostly blacks bought it. This was his remarks, "thanks Niggers for making me rich!" What we don't understand is the more we support bigots like these is the richer and more powerful they will get in this life hence, the sores of the black man will only get worse. It does not stop there, a well known black Indian cricketer spoke openly calling an Australian black cricketer a monkey and that is how silly it gets because obviously, he definitely forgot to look in the mirror before he opened his big mouth. The only good thing about this is that he apologized later. This is now the saying of a Chinese man, that the black man has small brain and a big penis while he the Chinese man is the opposite of that. Also, it has been said that if you want to hide something from a black man put it in a book. Now, I agree with that because most of us won't open a book much more to read it hence, we will always be stuck in reverse not knowing anything so we won't be able to move forward as a race.

The Holy Bible teaches that the Black Christ created all things beautiful so ugly which is the opposite of beautiful was created in the mind of human beings. Read (Ecclesiastes Ch. 3 vs 11). We are all different and created equally beautiful in the eyes of God so no human being should compare his physical self with another. The prejudice white man in his quest to try and prove his false sense of superiority started beauty contests in the US about one hundred years ago among young women. This contest is one of the biggest insults to the black woman because whenever she enters she has to physically prepare herself like a white woman or risk not getting a sponsor. For example, her hair has to be straight and we know normally that the hair of blacks is described in the Holy Bible to that of lambs wool so she has to use hair chemical to do the job while the white woman just comes natural. Why do we have to be always running down what the white man is doing and now seeing the black woman putting herself in all this discomfort because the chemicals that is used to straighten hair, burns the scalp. How many black women displaying their true blackness have won this contest since it started?

The mind is the most powerful thing there is and whatever we feed the mind with without a doubt will become a reality. You and I weren't around centuries or even thousands of years ago so if we are going to have an idea of what had taken place during those eras we will have to depend on the people who lived during those times, recorded events and passed it down through generations. The most authentic of all books is the Holy Bible, God's word and was written by inspired men. If the Holy Bible says something took place then it should readily be accepted with no arguments and if it didn't say something took place then it should be cast aside without even a discussion because you have to remember that this is God's word and God's word is final. When it comes to studying the Holy Bible you cannot speculate or allow your instinct to get in the way, nor can you debate the words of the black Christ. **Its either you accept it as it is or you don't.**

This is why it is important for us to read the Holy Bible for ourselves and stop taking the word of these misguided pastors who have trapped our minds because of how Christianity was presented to us. Our ancestors just listened, believed and fell in line by what was said by these wretched white pastors. This evil way of teaching the gospel have made some of us so ignorant that no matter how respected intellectual blacks try to show them the raw facts about their rich history, they just shut you out and continue with the garbage that was taught to them. But what is so sweet about the garbage that was taught them that they would literally say the most unkind things to those who try to open their eyes with the truth of the Holy Bible? The great Marcus Garvey says the only time the black man knows himself is when his back is against the wall. The black Christ died on the cross for us. Apart from Him, when our backs are against the wall, who will cry for us? What is troubling, they are so blinded by ignorance that they even taught their children all the garbage too. Then, we start to wonder why we have so many problems in the black communities. Today, some of them are still in line and in so doing trying to keep down their black brothers and sisters who are trying to uplift themselves out of a trapped situation.

If you don't stop listening to people who are guided by the devil you will never have any pride of your existence and you will never know for yourself the rich talent which exist within you. How can you call your brother man or answer to someone when they call you "Dog?" How can every time you dress to go anywhere your under wear is on display with your pants waist literally at your knees? We have gone from being the best dressed race in the 1970s to the sloppiest in the new millennium. The situation we are in now we cannot get any worse because we are already at the rock bottom. How can any decent woman go anywhere with you when you are dressed like that? How can you tattoo the picture of a serpent on your body and be proud of it when God cursed this creature in the Garden of Eden? All our black heroes dressed with pride so why can't we make them our role models?

While we are to read our Holy Bibles, we have to be very careful of these modern version Bibles going around because God is the same yesterday, today and forever and He didn't tell anyone to tamper or modernize His word, a matter of fact adding and subtracting from God's word is a serious sin. Most of these modernized versions are very strange and misleading because they have omitted the word **black** from their Bibles while trying to paint Christ even whiter.

# THE WORK PLACE

─── ─── ─── ─── ─── · ─── ─── ─── ─── ─── ─── ─── ───

It is said that your job is the most important thing to you because if you don't have a job you can't make any money and if you can't make any money you can't pay your bills and if you can't pay your bills life will be most miserable. This is how important your job is but this saying only goes for the person that lives within the law.

Where you work you must always respect your coworker position and qualification and encourage the teachings of the Black Christ because you are going to find workers among you who are too ambitious and are always pushing themselves further than they ought to be. If you could avoid them you would but because of the working environment you can't. This is where the teachings of the Black Christ come in because without Him your stress level is going to rapidly increase. The same workers that you eat, drink, laugh and communicate with at work are the same ones that are going to stab you in the back and try to make you lose your job because of their ambitions.

The black race is the most difficult set of people to supervise or organize because of their educational level and their determination to be willing slaves. Also, they are very disobedient to the teachings of the black Christ which will not argue well for them in the future. Right away we come back to education again and because of that we find ourselves being underpaid, over worked and discriminated against sometimes even by our own blacks. It makes the hypocrisy level among blacks at the work place alarmingly high. Then your mind starts to wonder off in time comparing where you work with the wretched slave plantation back then where you had field slaves and house slaves. Once you were a slave you have no pay to get but strangely, the house slaves loved the master and got favors because they constantly kept him informed with what is happening and when the master gets sick they get sick too while the field slaves hated the master and were always brutalized and never trusted.

When you look at your daily life sometimes you find yourself spending more time at the work place than your home so anywhere you work you must respect your boss whether you like him or not. Despite the loyalty that you should show to your boss to secure your employment status the work place can be the most challenging in your life. Most of the time, you have no thanks to get. You must not allow your boss to divide or set you against your fellow black man the way the Willie Lynch garbage said it must be done because divide and rule system of management is evil. Worst, if he is already under paying and over working you don't volunteer any unnecessary information to him because one day it will be used against you. If you are in a supervisory position, do not be the bearer of bad news only while the boss puts himself in position to be the bearer of all the good news to the workers. Remember the workers will not be so understanding, they will take the bad news in a wrong way and hate you when you are just carrying out the boss instructions. For professional reasons, tell no one your personal business because one day it might be used against you and costing you your job. Wherever you work you must be honest, loyal and flexible because once you accept the job you must perform to the best of your ability. You have to remember that a lot of people out there need jobs so don't put yourself in a position that you have to be job hunting in a very scarce job market.

There are some serious trends happening in the work place today as we speak. In spite of all the advertisement for you to attend college and further your education, a qualified black man was told at the work place when he applied for a job vacancy that whatever qualification he has does not matter there. On a salary scale, some people are paid more money than others doing the same job and some are always quicker to get a promotion with inferior qualification. Some ambitious blacks who are already employed at the company try to get ahead of the game so they pay their way back to college so they can attract higher salaries and have an edge on promotion when it is available. Well, not so says the bigot and his false blue eye white Jesus! Because in his company, for the black man to get a promotion he must show a willingness to cut his black brother's throat so most of the time the under qualified black man is promoted over the qualified black man. Then we are going to ask ourselves what sense does it make paying thousands of dollars going to school or even sending our children to school when snitching on our black brothers and sucking up to the boss is all that matters to get ahead. Some of us are so ignorant that even when our black brothers are not wrong we are willing to support an evil system that will make him pay a serious price for his academic achievements. So we see again why education and unity are so important. In bad mind situation like these we must trust in the black Christ and go to the Holy Bible for advice. The black Christ states in the Holy Bible that we should never be dismayed or loose courage because He is always with us and He will never fail us. Read (Deuteronomy Ch. 31 vs 6) and (Joshua Ch. 1 vs 9).

# WOLF IN SHEEP CLOTHING

▬ ▬ ▬ ▬ ▬ ▬ ▬ ▬ ▬ ▬ ▬ ▬

Once you accept and give your life to something you have to be very careful. You must do your own research of the Holy Bible and not only listen to what other people have to say. For example, look at a very influential white speaker like Jim Jones who posed as a minister of religion and was featured in the 1978 Jonestown massacre. He gave instruction to many people to commit suicide and they did. If the victims had done their proper research of the Holy Bible they would have seen that he was a wolf in sheep clothing, the devil disciple. The black Christ in the Holy Bible died for our sins so that we could have life. He never instructed anyone to commit suicide. Read (Isiah Ch. 41 vs 10) and (Jeremiah Ch. 29 vs 11).

In South Africa when the white missionaries went there they arrived with Bibles in their hands and the land was in the hands of the black man. As the years passed with a lot of twisted half truths and blatant lies from the prejudice white man there was a big swop where the black man ended up being fooled and trapped with the Bible in his hands and the white man ended up with the land. Only God knows the full truth of what really took place and there was nothing but decades of blood shed of the blacks in that country. Equal rights and justice did not come until the latter part of the twentieth century led by the great Nelson Mandela.

Look at what took place during slavery in the western hemisphere, white missionaries with Bibles and false teachings help to calm the slaves when they rebelled against oppression and kept them in slavery for several more decades before freedom came. The wicked white missionaries took full advantage of their illiteracy and taught them that they must forgive their slave masters and subject themselves to them. Now, this word forgive is one of the most misunderstood word by Christians even today. To forgive a person, they must totally stop doing a certain wicked act which affects you in various ways and show remorse. Once you are convinced that they have stopped and you are comfortable then you can forgive. You cannot forgive a person who consistently displays wicked acts against you over and over again because of your skin color or for no reason at all. If you are lucky to be getting away with your life every time they make an attempt, you have to avoid that person totally or defend yourself physically if you have to because they mean you no good. Also, the only master you must subject yourself to is the Black Christ of the Holy Bible.

All three incidents in this chapter have one thing in common, the false teachings of the blue eye white Jesus. In the Jones town massacre the people could read but in the other two the people could not so they listened to the devils disciples dressed in sheep clothing deceiving them with twisted half truths that they claim came from the Bible. These incidents again show that we are too trusting of people who mean us no good and claim to be Bible scholars. Some manipulating people are still doing the same thing today because we won't read the Bible to find the truth for ourselves.

When you think that we have learnt our lesson and to move on with our lives, a white preacher came on National television some years ago in the (1980s) and said that if he doesn't get several million dollars he is going to die. Now, this is several years after the incidents mentioned in this chapter and we still continue to be drawn into a situation where some of us black folks actually gave money to this white man and his family business called a church. Never give your hard earned money to any pastor who claims that he comes in the name of God and can afford to wear a different suite every day, with each suite costing more than the bed that you sleep on!

I wonder what has happened to all those church people who lost their jobs and their houses during the recession. What did the church with all those greedy pastors do for them? According to the Holy Bible the church is a place where the saints can gather and worship the black Christ in truth and in spirit. Christianity supposed to be a practical religion but why that practice is not a reality is because of the type of leadership in the form of pastors that it has. Let's take a look at a practical example. A church has for example, approximately one hundred members and ten of them lost their jobs and is about to lose their house. Now, what the black Christ would want the other ninety to do with the leadership of the pastor is to take care of the ten who are under pressure. A special collection must be collected every month and given to the members under pressure so they can pay their mortgage and have somewhere for them and their family to live comfortably. This must be continued without the greedy pastors dipping into the collection plate, until the members find another job because one of the worst things to happen to any human being is for them to lose their home.

We have a God given responsibility as parents to make sure that our children at no time at all must believe that there's peace and safety in anything that some people says and finding themselves trapped in any situation. It's for us as parents to teach our children only the truth because some decisions you make in life today will live with you and your generations for a very long time, sometimes too long.

# WITCHCRAFT

Throughout the entire Holy Bible the art of witchcraft, voodoo, obeah, black magic or whatever we want to call it have been condemned by the black Christ. This goes to show you that the ways of God is different, a much higher standard from the ways of man. People who practice witchcraft is always within themselves, trying to compete with the black Christ. Read (1Samuel ch.15 vs.23) (Exodus Ch.22 vs.18) (Leviticus ch.19 vs.31).

Another form of deception that the black man practice daily is superstition which is a practice of ignorance, fear of the unknown and thinking that magical things can happen if there is a certain practice. This ignorance is one of the main reasons why our minds are trapped and have found ourselves so far behind and try as we may we can't catch up. We keep holding on to this garbage and won't let go. Some of the ignorance that we believe and practice is if a person sneeze or walk under a ladder it can be bad luck or a person birthday falling on Friday 13th is a curse. Also, if you have an STD you can be cured if you have sex with a virgin, now, this is one of the most troubling one! These are just some of the garbage the black man has embedded in his mind from generation to generations and try as you may to convince him otherwise you 're just wasting your time. Seven days for the week the black man spends time reading and believing in horoscopes instead of reading and trusting in the Holy Bible. If we do not fear God and feed ourselves daily with the teachings of the black Christ we are going to end up serving the devil. Read in the Holy Bible (1 Peter Ch. 1 vs 13) (Romans Ch. 8 vs 5-7) (Deuteronomy Ch. 4 vs 19).

Ever wonder why no matter how hard we try, we are always finding ourselves well behind always trying to catch up in a system that is always eluding us? It's because of what we have embedded in our minds. Too much of us believe in witchcraft the way to self destruction and it has been so for centuries. What the black Christ curse, man cannot bless and we have to keep remembering that if we are going to hit the road to progress.

The Holy Bible teaches you that you can't serve two masters and the way of the black Christ is the only way to salvation so I don't see why we keep holding on to something that is evil and giving the devil too much say in our lives. We also have to remember that the Holy Bible teaches that witchcraft practice can bring serious curse on your generations. If witchcraft had the sort of power that we think it have we would not have been in slavery for so long because we inherited the craft from our African ancestors and it would not work against the slave master.

A black man lived all his life practicing witchcraft and one day he got sick and found himself in a hospital bed battling for his life. When he felt serious pain and smelt death hovering over his bed, surprisingly he did not call on his practice of witchcraft. He called on Christ to spare him. This goes to show that he knew all along in the back of his mind that the black Christ is the real Big Man in town but he chose to live a life of denial. A lot of us are in the same position but we have to learn that we might not be as lucky as him. His soul was saved from condemnation and many more can be if we just wake up and serve the black Christ. Witchcraft is the way of the devil so don't let it be too late before we find out.

The Holy Bible does not teach you to drink blood or physically harm anybody to prove your loyalty to the black Christ. The Holy Bible teaches you the conditioning of the mind through faith, it teaches you to love God, your neighbor and even your enemies. It also teaches forgiveness and to honor your parents.

The white man does not practice the art of witchcraft but that does not say anything because some of them are pagans or atheists which is just as bad, they do not believe in God.

# OUR CONSCIENCE

Our conscience is the part of us that distinguishes between right and wrong. If you want to know how right you are the Holy Bible must approve whatever you are doing, saying or thinking. If the Holy Bible does not approve then it is wrong and must not be condoned.

Over the centuries some serious cruelty was done to the black race by some white folks and all this was said to be done in the false blue eye white Jesus name with no remorse shown. It is also evident that some white folks believes and practice to be a way of life, to be a popular leader with the people you have to oppose the commandments of the black Christ. This is also evident that the false blue eye white Jesus is different from the black Christ of the Holy Bible. Why is this, the black Christ of the Holy Bible teaches that we must look at His works for evidence of the Father in Him. You see nothing but love and forgiveness in His actions while the same cannot be said for the false blue eye white Jesus. Read (John Ch. 14 vs 10-14) in the Holy Bible. Let us take a look at some of what was said and done by people with earthly power and see what the Holy Bible says in regard to them.

In the 1930s the Italian fascist leader Mussolini who was a close ally to Adolph "Lucifer" Hitler who together were supporters of the false blue eye white Jesus, planned an invasion to brutalize and destroy the black people of Ethiopia for no apparent reason. Before the invasion the entire Italian army was blessed by the pope at the time. All the guns, the tanks and the bombs of destruction were blessed in a way that we have never seen before. This blessing was done in the name of the false blue eye white Jesus hence, the Italian army was seen as a superior army to the one in Ethiopia. When the attack was launched the Italian army got the surprise of their lives and were thoroughly defeated by an inferior army and driven back by a leader who believed in the black Christ. The rest is history.

Who is this Pope? The Pope is said to be the head of Catholics International and in Catholics teaching, they claim that Peter a disciple of the black Christ was the first Pope. I have a problem with that because the Holy Bible teaches that Peter was married. Read (Matthew Ch.8 vs 14) (1 Cor. Ch.9 vs 5). **If Peter the first claimed Pope was married, where is the other Pope wife?** Where was the powerful voice of the pope during world war two (2) when thousands of decent people were thrown into gas chambers right under his nose? Also, it is observed recently that the statue or painting of a black Jesus is on display in some Catholic Churches in some countries. I have a big problem because these people claimed that they are great bible scholars, how are they just knowing the truth? **What are they up to this time?**

Some years ago a famous white religious world leader from Italy said that heaven is a state of mind. The Holy

Bible teaches that heaven is a place. Read (John Ch.14 vs 1-7). Who are you going to believe, the Holy Bible or man? If heaven wasn't a place, where would believers of the black Christ go to be comforted in the next life after being oppressed all their lives by people who practice wickedness as a way of life? The black Christ assured Christians that He has gone to prepare a place where there will be no more death, no more pain and no more hunger and the black Christ does **NOT TELL LIES!**

The latest ambitious plan of the white man in his quest to control is to have a one world order with his false blue eye white Jesus at the head. In this plan an electronic chip will be planted in an individual to identify and track them anywhere in the world they are. Not so says the black Christ of the Holy Bible! The black Christ teaches that He is the shepherd and once you are a part of His flock He can identify you anywhere in the world you are. He does not need an electronic chip to identify anybody. Read in the Holy Bible (John Ch. 10 vs 14). So again you see for yourself how dangerous life can be if you don't read the Holy Bible and see that the black Christ is totally different from the false blue eye white Jesus.

Up to the late sixties the mormons a so called religious group in the US refused people of a darker shade skin tone to be members of their congregation. Thank God things have changed because according to them the black man is now welcomed. This religious group have written their own Bible and claimed in it that Christ appeared in the United States. If the black Christ of the Holy Bible was to appear in the United States and knocked on a Mormon door, they would slam the door in His face and called Him an "**Imposter**" because He would be black. On the other hand the false blue eye white Jesus would be welcomed with open arms. Right away you can compare the false blue eye white Jesus in their Bible with the Black Christ of the Holy Bible. They claim that they have forgiven black people but what have they forgiven us for, to be BLACK?

Another famous white religious leader said that you must love God and your neighbor. Yes! I agree with that because it is found in the Holy Bible. Read (Matthew Ch.22 vs 34-40) but what kind of honesty and truth comes from his heart with that quotation from the Bible. After all the wretchedness that was done by them over the centuries it is very difficult for the black man to believe anything from the mouth of some white folks about the love of God and the love of his neighbor. Some white men are atheist so how can you love someone that you don't think exist and you hate the black man so you will never love your neighbor. Definitely, somebody is not practicing what they are preaching.

The United States of America was built on a Christian foundation. One only has to go back to the beginning when the settlers left Europe and came to the New World. When they came they came in groups and anywhere they settled they had a church where they could worship. What made the United States of America so great today is because of the foundation that was laid with the Holy Bible as the main book of authority but somewhere along the line atheism has taken over and dominated the country with man totally forgetting the blessing they came to the New World with. They started to enslave people, the Bible has been taken out of schools and Easter which recognizes the crucifixion and resurrection of the black Christ is seen as an ordinary day. We have to remember that the resurrection of Christ from the dead is the most important part of Christianity. It's the part that gives man hope and without hope life is meaningless. Sadly, more homage and respect is paid to Halloween which is a holiday that celebrates witches, demons and other spirits. The answer to all this is that no blue eye white Jesus was ever crucified so the importance of Easter was shifted to Halloween as a bigger celebration.

In the United States, the most vicious white extremists organization the KKK were ardent supporters of this false blue eye white Jesus. For decades, this extremist group was responsible for the killing of thousands of innocent blacks and not one of its members were ever convicted for murder until the latter part of the twentieth century. Most of the murders that they committed were done in plain view of several people and when they were arrested and taken to court by their friends, they were released by an all white juror. Only whites could judge another white person in those days and today, you still have people working underground to bring back those days. That's why it is important for blacks to know their history and stand on their own feet and not to look for any favors from anyone.

Over the centuries some white folks from generations to generations up until this day have caused pain and suffering both physically and mentally to be a way of life for the black man. It has been so severe sometimes that some blacks within themselves expressed openly that they were sorry to be black and asked themselves, what kind of place are they living in? Just a few years ago when the black man defended himself against the vicious cruelty against him by some white folks, the black man who was the victim was branded as the criminal and either killed or imprisoned. How on God's earth can any human being practice all this wickedness and sleep comfortably in his bed without his conscience giving him a hard time? But, does the prejudice white man have a conscience or anybody at all who worships this false blue eye white Jesus?

Once you are an atheist you do not believe in life after death so the way of life of some white folks is evident he craves after money and couldn't care less about anybody who does not have the same skin tone as him. The Holy Bible teaches about life after death (2Cor. Ch.5 vs 10 and Heb. Ch.9 vs 27-28). **If there is no life after death it means that man has no hope and wickedness has been victorious.** For those who read the Holy Bible you will learn that the Black Christ is not a liar and He is the only one on record that has never sinned.

These are just some of the reminders that the interpretation of the Bible by some white folks is different from the truth that we read and the God they serve looks different from the one we serve. Special note, No blue eye white Jesus was ever mentioned in the Holy Bible. A true description of Christ can be found in the King James Version of the Holy Bible and not in the new modern versions which deliberately erased the word black from their version. King Solomon son of David both descendants of the tribe of Judah were described as black when you read (Songs of Solomon Ch.1 vs 5). Jeremiah a descendant of the tribe of Benjamin described as black when you read (Jeremiah Ch.8). Both Judah and Benjamin were brothers from the same father Jacob. Christ is also a descendant of the tribe of Judah is described as black when you read (Revelation Ch.1

vs 9-20). Christ feet is described to that of burning brass and we know how black brass is when it is burned and His hair is described to that of lambs wool. Only the black race has wooly hair. This false blue eye white Jesus only came on the scene during slavery to promote a false sense of superiority by the white man. Before slavery, all images of God known to man was black. The Holy Bible teaches that when you pray and have faith in the black Christ he will never turn His back on you and will sooner or later answer your prayer. Some of us black folks who have lost faith in prayer because your prayer is never answered is because we are not focusing on the truth of the Holy Bible. (John Ch. 15 vs 5-7).

Who is this false blue eye white Jesus? I have to ask this question because most things the white man does is done in his name and it is also evident that what the false blue eye white Jesus does is the opposite of what the black Christ of the Holy Bible teaches. Also, it is interesting to know that this false blue eye white Jesus is the only god in the world that entertains SAME SEX MARRIAGE. The marriage officers holding Bible in their hands and claims that they are conducting these same sex marriages can only be representing the false blue eye white Jesus because the black Christ of the Holy Bible condemns this behavior. Read (Leviticus Ch.20 vs 13) (Romans Ch.1 vs 26 -27). Let me make myself clear, I have nothing against a homosexual because they are human beings but what I think they should do in order to gain maximum respect from the public is to form their own churches. Call it **"Faggots for Christ"** if they want but don't bully your way into a situation which you say is hostile to you in the Holy Bible. I am and will always be a true believer in the teachings of the Holy Bible and nothing can change that. The Holy Bible teaches us that God created Adam and Eve and not Adam and Steve, therefore, marriage supposed to be a union between man and woman. The Holy Bible also teaches us that God told them to go and multiply and it is evident from what we have seen and heard in history two bulls cannot multiply. Read (Genesis Ch. 9 vs 7) and (Genesis Ch. 1 vs 28). God does not go back on His word and when He tells us to do something it's a command which is an order. God's word cannot be negotiated and He does not beg us anything hence, disobediences to His orders carry serious consequences. The rate of how these people are growing and using their evil money to bully their way into society, the US has to be very careful that they are not compared to Sodom and Gomorrah in the Holy Bible. Read (Genesis Ch. 19). You ever wonder if everybody was to become gay what would happen to the population of this world.

There is a well publicize man made argument going around that children that is raised by same sex couples grow up to be normal. If any truth is in this, it mean that someone is trying to say the Holy Bible is a lie and we who are believers in the Holy Bible know that the Holy Bible which is God's word stands supreme and can't lie. This is where the false white blue eye Jesus is deceiving them because if you have children growing up in a situation where they see their parents who are of the same sex hugging and kissing in front of them affectionately and at then locking themselves away in the same bedroom can only become one of two things. Its either they become just like their parents or they grow up in some cases having a permanent sick stomach. Children live what they learn and the Black Christ of the Holy Bible was very specific when it comes to children. Read (Matthew Ch. 19 vs 13 – 15) in the Holy Bible.

Also on another point of view, the United States while giving the go ahead by law for same sex marriage even when it is condemned by the Holy Bible, there is a manmade law which stops men from having more than one wives. This is interesting because the Holy Bible does not condemn this practice and this was a regular practice by men of God in the Holy Bible. The black Christ says in the Holy Bible that He is here to fulfil the laws and not to change it. Read (Matthew Ch. 5 vs 17). So why is man trying to Bless what God Curse and at the same time sending people to prison who try to live like the great kings of the Holy Bible by having more than one wife? If a man can afford to have more than one wife at any one time there should not be a problem to man because the Holy Bible does not see a problem in it. However, if you are married and have sex outside of that marriage, then that is when the problem comes in. **The Black Christ of the Holy Bible is the same yesterday, today and forever and He had no problem with having more than one wife yesterday, so what are you trying to tell me that God has gone back on His words today. I'm sorry but God does not go back on His words.**

# HOLY PRESENCE

Being in the presence of the Black Christ can be very dangerous if you are not committed according to the Holy Bible. Read (Exodus Ch.28 vs 31-35)(Leviticus Ch. 16 vs 2-4)(Acts Ch. 5 vs 1-11).

These above Bible verses teach us that the Israelite priest had to come clean when they were in the presence of God. The Holy Bible book of Acts teaches about Ananias and his wife Sapphira who were both killed by God when they lied in His presence. We tend to take His presence for granted but we have to remember as kind, loving and forgiving as the black Christ is, His wrath can be very **catastrophic**. We also have to remember that He does not accept any form of gift from pagans nor will He entertain any form of disobedience from His children. Read (1 Samuels Ch.15 vs 10-34). This Chapter will teach you how Saul was removed from being King of Israel because of disobedience to God and what Samuel did to the pagan king named Agag after he read him the charges.

God's first recorded home in the Holy Bible is the Garden of Eden a place of paradise. He later created man in

His own image to represent Him, then God created woman to be man's helper and partner. Because of disobedience both man and woman was expelled from the Garden of Eden by God. Suppose Adam had apologized and begged forgiveness for his sin instead of trying to hide from God to cover his guilt. Wouldn't things have been different today, seeing that we serve a merciful and forgiving God who loved us so dearly? All the pain and suffering that the human race encountered over the centuries was because of the sin of Adam. Today we are still disobedient to God's word in the Holy Bible, everything we do is the opposite of what the Black Christ command, yet we want to see a better way of life. Those of us who read the Holy Bible will know that God do not dwell in sin. One day He is going to return because He does not lie and He is going to take obedient believers to His home.

The Holy Bible teaches us that your body is the temple of God. Read (1 Corinthians Ch.3 vs 16-17) and (1 Corinthians Ch. 6 vs 19).In view of these verses the body must be kept clean at all times and in light of this we have to be very careful that what we consume must not harm the body. For example, illegal drugs and alcohol the two most deadly addictions should not be consumed.

If a man and woman are not deeply in love and serious, do not take a marriage vow because when you come into God presence and take any vow you have to live by that vow all the days of your life. What we see happening in today's world, a person will get married today and the following month they will claim that they don't love their spouse any more so they file for a divorce. While in another instance a person might not be in love but they love the money that their spouse has so they get married. A few months later when all the money is gone they file for divorce. The Holy Bible teaches us that the only arguably grounds for divorce is adultery. Read (Matthew Ch. 19 vs 9). People that do these things must be doing it out of ignorance because if you read the Holy Bible and see how dangerous the presence of God is I doubt if you would even try it. While you can trick or hide from man you cannot trick or hide from God. Why most people sin so often and think they are getting away with it, it's because of God mercy and patience but beware, we have seen in the Holy Bible where His patience ran out and His wrath went against His chosen people the Israelites and scattered them. Read (Jeremiah Ch. 9 vs 16) (1 Kings Ch. 14 vs 15).

The more you read the Holy Bible is the more aware you will be to the truth and the more you will understand the ways of the black Christ. God is so merciful that it's not what you were but what you are today that matters. As I said before, as kind, loving and forgiving as the black Christ is, His wrath can be catastrophic! **No human being can defend himself against the wrath of God**.

The false blue eye white Jesus teaches that when you have money in abundance you are blessed. Not so says the black Christ in the Holy Bible because a lot of ungodliness is involved when accumulating wealth. Read (Hebrews Ch.13 vs 1-6) (1 Timothy Ch.6 vs 10) (Ecclesiastes Ch.5 vs 10) (Acts Ch.8 vs 20) (Philippians Ch.4 vs 19). Additional proof is the countries in northern Europe which have some of the strongest economy in the world yet they are among the highest when it comes to suicide rate in the world. The question I want to ask, why is there so much suicide in these countries when they are better off than most countries financially? Also the percentage of the population that believes in God is very low. This goes to show that money don't bring total happiness so the teaching of the false blue eye white Jesus about being blessed when you have an abundance of money is garbage. There is no redemption in this false blue eye white Jesus so his way is not the way of the Holy Bible. You notice that the people who have a lot of money and believe in the false white Jesus, the more money they have is the more they want and the more wretched they are. The love of God is replaced by the love of money. The Israelite Kings were wealthy but don't watch that their wealth was given and controlled by God so they were always thankful. Read (Mark Ch. 12 vs 38-44) and (Luke Ch. 16 vs 19-31) for perfect examples of blessing.

The Holy Bible also warns that many will come in His name. Read (Matthew Ch.24 vs 3-8) (Mark Ch.13 vs 3-8). Just read the Holy Bible and compare the teachings of the Holy Bible with the way of life of these so called religious leaders. These people have brought the devils interpretation to the Holy Bible and thinking within themselves that they can twist the word of God to suit their evil life style.

# ONE RACE

━━ ━━ ━━ ━━ ━━ ━━ ━━ ━━ ━━ ━━ ━━ ━━ ━━ ━━

One race was created by the Black Christ and that's the human race and its God business what color or built He wants to make them in. God created all of us equal in His sight to be kind and loving to each other. Our duty as human beings is to serve Him with all our hearts and soul and to be totally obedient to His commandments. He also wants us to live in peace with all and let vengeance be His alone. Read (Romans Ch.12 vs 18-19). The more we are rebellious to the black Christ and His commandments, is the more life itself will become unbearable.

We are all brothers and sisters whether we like it or not and God alone has the power to judge whatever you do or say. Before we start judging the behavior of another individual we must visualize ourselves in that person position first and try to understand what they went through. Then we can start the process of forgiving so all wounds can heal because only then Godliness can flow. The Holy Bible also teaches that life is a mist that appears for a little while then vanishes. Read (James Ch.4 vs 12 - 17). Man has no power to judge because in man there is too much sin. Read (1 John Ch. 1

vs 8). Only the Black Christ when He lived in the flesh is without sin.

No human being has the power of knowing what's going to happen next except those who are specially inspired by God. Imagine what man would be like if he knew from before what would happen next.

According to Paul letters in the New Testament, the Black Christ should have returned already but the Black Christ also stated that He will come like a thief in the night which means no one knows exactly when. Read (2 Peter Ch. 3 vs 10). What we have to do in the meantime is make ourselves prepared for His return and when He returns those who lived on Easy Street and turn their backs on Him will be in torment while those who struggled and worshipped Him will live on Easy Street.

## CLOSING PRAYER

FOR THE LOVE OF GOD THE TRUE BLACK CHRIST, THE MESSIAH OF THE HOLY BIBLE, I PRAY THAT ONE DAY YOU WILL GIVE US THE STRENGTH TO BE OBEDIENT AND HATE WHAT IS EVIL AND LOVE WHAT IS RIGHTEOUS AND YOU'LL SOLVE ALL THE PROBLEMS OF THOSE WHO BELIEVE IN YOUR LOVE, MERCY AND FORGIVENESS WHETHER THEY ARE BLACK OR WHITE. I PRAY THESE THINGS IN JESUS THE BLACK CHRIST PRECIOUS NAME.

## AMEN